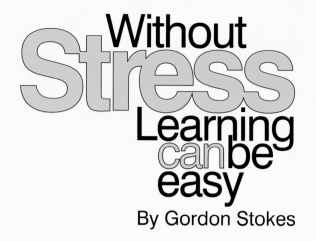

Without Stress Learning can be easy

By Gordon Stokes

During the author's early school years, he had an initial learning block. Not recognized as such, he was labeled "dumb" or "backward." Mocked by his peers and despaired of at home, for a time, he bought into that image. He is now President of an educational corporation that trains both professionals and the general public internationally how to correct learning disabilities through stress reduction skills.

Without Stress Learning can be easy

By Gordon Stokes

This book
is dedicated
to everyone.

We
really
CAN LEARN!

Published by
TACTICS
2000 W. Magnolia Blvd. #201
Burbank, California 91506, USA

ISBN: 0-918993-81-4
Library of Congress No.96-90306
Copyright©1996 by Gordon Stokes
Design, Layout, Illustrations by Serge Pichii

Introduction

Over the last 10 years, thousands of school children and adults have benefited extensively doing the exercises presented in this book. This method is being used in Europe, including Russia and the Slavic countries. People in other countries such as Japan, South America, Australia, Africa, and Israel are also benefiting. The stress of our times creates much of the hyper-activity in our children. Many that are taking the drug Ritalin find they don't need it as much or at all after doing *these exercises.*

To the parents:
Although most middle graders will be able to read and understand this book, it will be helpful if you do the exercises with them. Teaching primary graders the exercises can help them to get a good start in school without the stress that causes so many learning problems. Doing the exercises for 30 days can make a remarkable change in your child's or young adult's school work and behavior.

To the teachers:
Many of the following exercises can be used in the classroom by having everyone do them. For teachers in special education you'll find that "slow learners" reduce their stress on learning and progress faster.

Many of us get learning

b

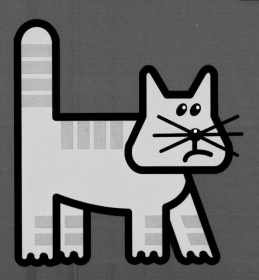

ocks

These blocks can show themselves when you reverse numbers or letters when you write. Blockages can make you forget answers you already know when you are taking a test. It can mean that you have a lot of trouble reading out loud. You might forget how to spell words correctly. Blocks can even cause you to forget what you have read. After we tell you how you get learning blockages, we will show you some exercises that can help you get rid of them, so learning is easier.

Table of contents

Magic points to rub
to help you
think better

How to
improve
your writing

What to do
if reading
makes you
tired or sleepy

What to do
every day
to help learning
and your
coordination

Getting better
on your
tests

Cover

**Avoidance
can be
a learning
block**

Once a shark was put in a large pool of water with a glass wall down the middle. The shark could not get to the other side of the pool even though it could see through the glass wall. The caretakers put food on the opposite side of the glass wall and when the shark went to get the food it bumped its nose against this glass wall. It went for the food a second time and bumped its nose against the wall again. Then it tried a third time without success. After that, the shark only swam in circles not going near the glass wall. When the wall was removed, the shark did not change its behavior. It would not try to go to the opposite side of the pool, even for food. In the shark's mind, the glass wall was still there. In order to keep the shark from starving, the caretakers had to put the food on the shark's side of the pool.

This shark's behavior is an AVOIDANCE block. It avoided being hurt again. AVOIDANCE is a type of learning block. Avoidance could be when we say we are sick and can't go to school because we have a test that day.

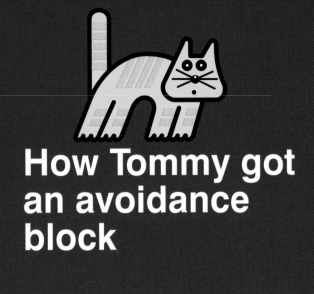

How Tommy got an avoidance block

Tommy was on his way to school, and he passed by a house with a BIG, black dog. The black dog barked and lunged at him. The dog frightened him so much that he would not go by that house to get to school. Tommy avoided meeting the dog that frightened him.

As Tommy grew older, he forgot about what happened with the big black dog when he was a small boy. Now, whenever Tommy sees a dog, he feels uneasy, and avoids going near it.

This is an AVOIDANCE block again.

School can cause learning blocks

The teacher called on Susan to read in front of her classmates. Susan made a mistake because she didn't know how to say a new vocabulary word on the page. When she heard the class laugh, she felt very embarrassed and started making even more reading mistakes.

The next time she was called upon to read in front of the class, Susan's body remembered how she felt when she made the mistake before. Her face became red and hot. She became confused before she even started reading in front of the room.

When she did read she made more mistakes. She felt even more embarrassed this time while standing in front of the room and reading. Now, Susan does not want to read in front of the class at all. When she knows she will have to read in front of the class, she tells her mother that she doesn't feel well enough to go to school that day. This is another AVOIDANCE block, just like the shark avoiding the glass wall and Tommy avoiding the big dog.

Let me tell you a secret.

Wouldn't it be wonderful to have someone looking over your shoulder that could tell you anything you want to know. Someone who knows how you feel and could advise you on what is best to do in all situations. Well, you do have someone. It's your REAL SELF. Read this closely and you'll know why your REAL SELF can help you if you'll only listen.

Your real self knows when you're angry. If this were not so, how do you know when you're angry? You might say, "I know when I'm angry!" Yes, and it is only your real self that knows it. Your false self is being angry and your real self knows it. Your real self knows when you're sad. Your false self is being sad. It's like having your real self on your shoulder whispering in your ear. The real self comes out to play when you're happy and confident. This is the self that knows how to read well, and is not afraid of dogs.

It is the false self that reminds you that you were chased by a black dog and so now you are nervous around dogs—especially black ones! It is the false self that reminds you about your reading in front of the class and being laughed at by your class mates. This is the false self that reminds you that you don't want to read in front of anyone or maybe not read at all. You may not even see the words on the page because your false self felt embarrassed when you read in front of a group. You may not spell well because it was words that caused your false self emotional pain.

Your false self remembers that once it wasn't easy to catch a ball so now your false self doesn't like sports. You don't even want to try. This is your false self that is BLOCKED.

When we remove the blocks from our false self, our real self, which is always with us will be in charge.

Now we know some reasons why we are not good in school or why we may even hate to go to school. Using our real self, we can do something about it. Our experiences might be happy or they might be sad. We can do certain exercises to change the ones we don't like.

Two things happen when we experience something. One is the experience itself; the other is the feeling we have about the experience.

We can't change the experience, but our real self can change the feelings we have about it. Once we change the feelings, the experience has no more power over us.

Tommy had the experience of being chased by the black dog, and he has the feeling of fear about being chased. If Tommy changes the frightened feeling, he won't be afraid of dogs when he sees them.

How to change our feelings about experiences that happened in the past

If Susan doesn't feel embarrassed when she reads, she will read better and not be afraid of the words on the page. Changing our feelings can get rid of these blocks.

Hold your head, or have someone you like hold your head, the same way as is shown in the picture. Then do the following exercises which are very easy because you only need to imagine something. These exercises will help you to change the feelings you don't like about your experiences.

Correction Exercises

If you have had an unpleasant experience, such as being chased by a black dog, being laughed at by your class, having a fight with your best friend or anything else that happened to you that you didn't like, there is something you can do. You can also use this for things you might be afraid of doing, like giving a report in front of the room.

Place one hand on your forehead, the other hand on the back of your head and close your eyes. Remember the unpleasant experience that happened to you like a picture in your mind. Or you can imagine something that you might be afraid to do. You can put everything into the picture, such as the black dog, the teacher or the friend you had a fight with.

Now create a frame around the picture and pay very close attention to it. Is it a big frame or a small one? What color is it? Does the frame have any decorations on it? When the frame is very clear in your mind, change the frame to one you like just as much or more than the first one. Change the size of the frame; if the frame was small, make it bigger. Change the color of the frame. If it was blue, make it yellow or any other color you like. Change the decorations on the frame. If it was plain, make it fancy. If it was fancy make it plain.

What to do if you are afraid of something

Now take a deep breath.

Open your eyes and remove your hands from your forehead and the back of your head. You don't have to look at the picture again. You will find that changing the frame will change the picture and how you FEEL about it. You may be surprised the next time you see your teacher–she or he won't be so frightening to you. Neither will the dog, or anything else that you put in the picture.

Remember, you can do this at any time, even while something frightening is happening to you. Just put one hand on your forehead and the other hand on the back of your head, and you will feel more comfortable.

Magic points to rub to help you think better

Do you remember listening to a radio that had so much static on it you could barely hear the song? It could be the dial on the radio needed adjusting so the sound was clearer. Sometimes you can be a little out of adjustment, and things in your head are not clear. Sometimes you don't hear or understand what is being said. You may even feel confused. If you feel this way sometimes, the Magic Points may help you. These points are on our body and when we rub them, our minds are clearer and we hear and see better. The points are located on the front and back of your body. You can rub them with one hand while putting the other hand on your navel (belly button). Rub all the points as shown in pictures 1, 2 and 3. Now, change hands and do it again. See these points on your body shown in the picture. This will balance any static energy in your body, just like adjusting the radio dial.

Many times you don't read well because your mind and body may be confused. Rubbing these points may help you read better and learn easier.

① ② ③

Try the following experiment:

Pick up one of your favorite books and read a paragraph or two from it out loud. Listen to yourself read. Notice how easy or difficult it is for you to read. If you stumble across words or you were not able to remember what you read, do the following exercise.

Be sure you read out loud BEFORE you do this exercise. Then put your book down. Place one hand on your navel and with your other hand, rub the two magic points just below your breast bone as shown in drawing number 1. At the same time, move your eyes from left to right, then right to left and continue moving them back and forth while you say the ABC's out loud. Say the entire alphabet, and do not move your head when you move your eyes. Now change your hands and do the same movements. Rub the magic points, move your eyes back and forth and say the ABC's out loud. Pick up your book and read it again. Notice the difference. Did the words seem easier to read? Did your voice sound different? Even a small change indicates you are getting better.

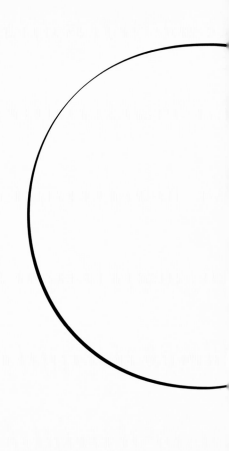

How to
Improve Your
Writing

Write several sentences on a large piece of paper. Do not print. Then put your pencil down. Look at your writing. Notice how even or uneven your letters are. How easy was it for you to write? The next exercise helps you coordinate your eyes and your hands so they work easier together.

Draw in the air a large figure 8 turned on its side. It will look like this:

To do this, place your arms out straight in front of you with your hands together and thumbs touching to make a hole you can see through. Look through the hole you made with your hands and draw a large figure 8, on its side, in the air. Keep your arms straight and make the figure 8 very large. Be sure to keep looking through the hole you have made with your fingers as you draw the figure 8. Do this exercise nine complete times, using your whole body.

Now with your first finger on the palm of your other hand outline a figure 8, placed on its side nine times, following with your eyes. Next, switch to the other palm and draw the same figure 8 nine more times.

Now place one hand on your forehead and the other on the back of your head, close your eyes and imagine a large chalk board. Draw a figure 8 on its side on this large imaginary chalk board in your mind nine times.

Take another piece of paper and write several sentences on the paper just as you did before. Is it easier to write this time? Does your writing look different from the other writing you made? If this exercise made an improvement, do this entire exercise every day before you go to school.

Sometimes our eyes get tired when we read for a long time, and it is difficult to remember what we have read. Read several pages from a book. Ask yourself "what did I read?" Can you remember?

Put your book down and do the following exercise: Look straight ahead and without moving your head, move your eyes as far as you can to the left, then to the right, then straight up, and straight down. Next, close your eyes and do the same eye movements keeping your eyes closed. Now do the next exercise.

What to do if reading makes you tired or sleepy

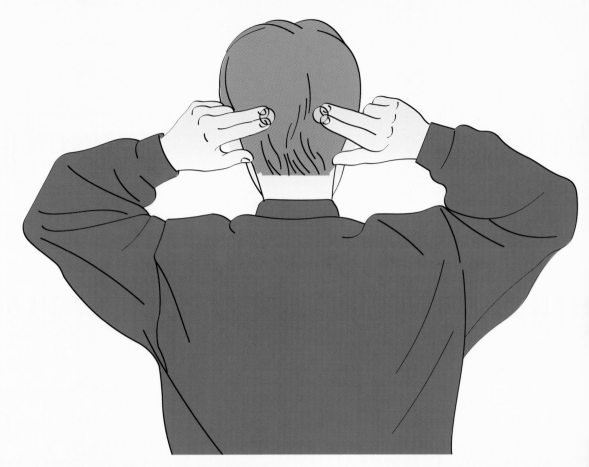

Now with your eyes open, rub the special eye points on the back of your head while you move your eyes as you did before. These eye points can be found on the same level as the top of your ears on the back of your head. Look at the picture for the location. You may find these two points are slightly indented. Keep rubbing the points on the back of your head as you move your eyes left, right, straight up, straight down, straight ahead. Next, close your eyes and move your eyes as you did before, while rubbing the eye points again. Now pick up your book and read again. Does the reading seem easier? Ask yourself what you read.

What to do every day to help learning and your coordination

Our brain has two halves. The half on the right side for the most part controls the left side of the body. The half on the left side controls the right side of the body. If you do the next exercise EVERY DAY, it will help you coordinate both sides of your brain. We call this exercise CROSS PATTERNING. March in place by raising your right arm and left leg. Then use the left arm and right leg. Do this 9 times alternating sides. Then change and raise your arm and leg on the same side, alternating sides and continue for 9 times. Then change again marching in place using opposite arm and leg for 9 times.

Repeat this exercise changing from the same side to the opposite side at least 9 times. End with the opposite side, right arm and left leg. You can also use music as you do this exercise. This will help both halves of your brain to work together which will help your learning ability and your coordination. You will find that you do better in sports as well as your other school work if you do CROSS PATTERNING every day. When you get really good at it, you can say the alphabet aloud or sing while doing this.

Getting better on your tests

Most of us think taking a test is one of life's scariest experiences. We feel we are being judged when we don't get good grades. Our parents expect good grades from us. So do our teachers. It is tough enough doing all the studying in order to do well on the test. We feel even worse when we do all that studying, and then when we look at the test, we can't remember the answers. While we stare at the questions on the test, it's as though there is a wall separating what we learned from what we can remember.

Here is a way of helping you relax when you know you will be taking a test. Place one hand on your forehead and the other hand on the back of your head as you already learned to do. Think of the day you will take the test. Imagine in your mind walking into the room where you will take the test. Look at the pictures on the wall. See the other students getting ready to take their tests.

Next, in your mind, watch the teacher hand out the test papers. One after the other, the students take their papers and start to work. Now take your paper. As you do, notice if the teacher is wearing any rings or other jewelry. What kind of shoes is the teacher wearing—are they in good condition or do they need a shine? Can you smell if the teacher is wearing any perfume or cologne?

Now, still in your mind, look at the test and see how many questions you have to answer. Go over the list in your mind as if you were taking the test and first answer all the questions that you know for sure. Skip any you are not sure about. When you finish with the ones you can answer right away, go back and review the questions you were not so sure of. Ask yourself, "What kind of person made up these questions, and what kind of an answer does that person want me to give?"

Then pick one answer and think of two or more possibilities. Put down your strongest impression. Next, do the same for the second question you weren't sure about. If nothing comes to mind, skip it for now and continue with another question. When you've reached the end, take another look at the questions that remain unanswered and write down whatever comes to your mind.

Now you've finished the test. Take a deep breath, go up to the teacher and hand in the test, knowing that you did well and much better than you expected. Imagine yourself feeling good and smiling. Repeat this entire process three times, then take a deep breath.

It is best to do this exercise the night before your test. Doing this in your mind three times is like taking the test three times. It relieves the stress of taking the test, and you will be able to think much better. You can also do the above exercise in practicing sports. Your body will respond as if you were on the basketball court, swimming, or even practicing the piano.

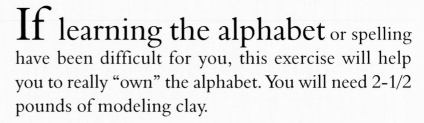

Working with Clay

If learning the alphabet or spelling have been difficult for you, this exercise will help you to really "own" the alphabet. You will need 2-1/2 pounds of modeling clay.

Look up at the picture of the alphabet in lower case letters. See the "a" and then make this lower case "a" with your modeling clay. Next do the "b." Continue making the letters with clay all the way through the entire alphabet. Let them dry. You may even want to paint them.

Lets talk about words. Letters make up words. We learn words only in our mind. Making clay models of the letters gets more of your senses involved and triggers different neurons in different parts of your brain. Neurons are small electrical currents that help you remember. Practicing with the letters this way will help you learn and remember words.

You can use the clay with numbers too.

1234567890

opqrstuvwxyz

NOW that you are getting smarter, you don't need to listen to your false self. Each time you do the exercises you will get better and better and you will be able to listen to your real self. Your real self is going to help you do better in school, have more fun with your friends, and help you to discover the smart you.